SUPER CITIES!

LOUISVILLE

by Lois Sepahban

arcadia
CHILDREN'S BOOKS

Published by Arcadia Children's Books
A Division of Arcadia Publishing
Charleston, SC
www.arcadiapublishing.com

Super Cities is a trademark of Arcadia Publishing, Inc.

First published 2023

Manufactured in the United States of America.

ISBN 978-1-4671-9895-0

Library of Congress Control Number: 2022950475

Notice: The information in this book is true and complete to the best of our knowledge. It is offered without guarantee on the part of the author or Arcadia Publishing. The author and Arcadia Publishing disclaim all liability in connection with the use of this book.

Produced by Shoreline Publishing Group LLC
Santa Barbara, California
Designer: Patty Kelley

Contents

WELCOME TO

Louisville!

Louisville, Kentucky

River City, Derby City, or Falls City—whatever you want to call it, Louisville, Kentucky, has it all! Kentucky's largest city sits along the Ohio River near a limestone formation that is home to amazing fossils. Louisville also has awesome parks and is home to the world's most famous horse race—the Kentucky Derby! World class museums feature art, history, and more. And you won't see the world's largest baseball bat anywhere but Louisville, the home of the Slugger!

FAST FACTS
Louisville, Kentucky
POPULATION: 628,594
FOUNDED: 1779
NICKNAMES:
Derby City, River City,
Falls City, the 'Ville
AREA:
61 square miles
PRONUNCIATION NOTES:
If you want to sound like a local,
you'll say LOO-a-vul.

Louisville is not as old as some other cities in the eastern or southern United States, but it's managed to pack a lot of history in since it was founded in 1779. Its handy location on the river has helped it grow to become a regional hub. From a place that was once on the edge of the frontier, Louisville has become a world center for businesses, tourists, horseracing fans, and more.

See you in the 'Ville!

LOUISVILLE: Map It!

The Mississippi River is in (roughly) the center of the United States and forms the westernmost boundary of the state of Kentucky. Follow the river north from the Gulf of Mexico until it reaches the Ohio River, and then travel eastward along the Ohio River—and there it is, the city of Louisville.

Long before it was called Louisville, people lived along the banks of the Ohio River. The river is shallow here, making it a perfect place for boats to stop and a city to grow. Louisville spreads east and west along the south side of the river, directly across from the state of Indiana, to cover an area of 61 square miles.

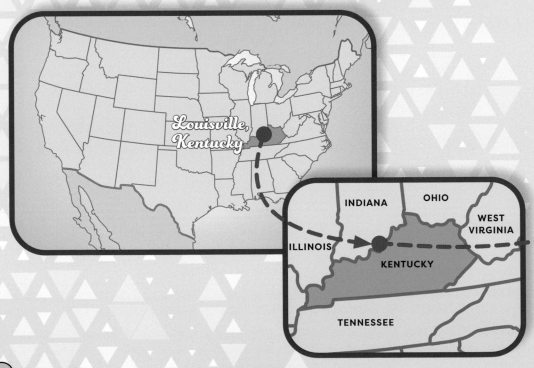

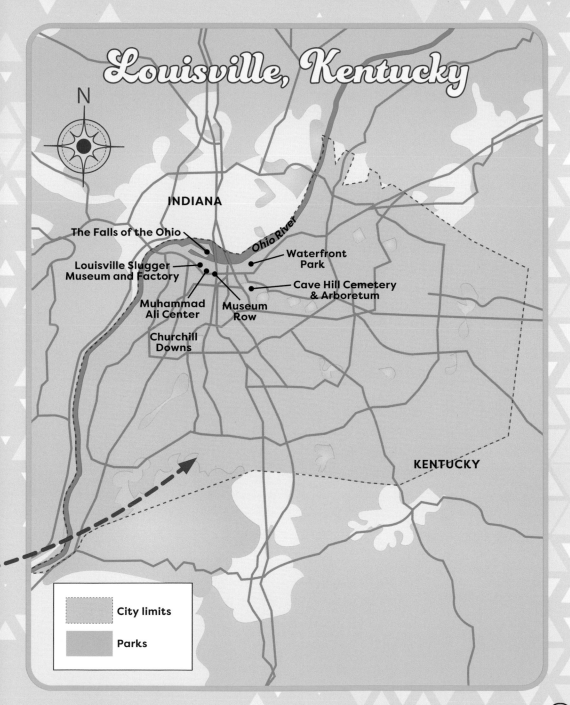

Louisville, Kentucky

INDIANA

The Falls of the Ohio

Ohio River

Waterfront Park

Louisville Slugger Museum and Factory

Cave Hill Cemetery & Arboretum

Muhammad Ali Center

Museum Row

Churchill Downs

KENTUCKY

City limits

Parks

Naming Louisville

In 1778, during the American Revolution, General George Washington sent Lieutenant Colonel George Rogers Clark, along with 150 men, to attack British forts along the Ohio River. Around 60 civilians traveled with them.

On May 27, 1778, Clark and his company landed on an island in the Ohio River just across from modern-day Louisville. Clark and the soldiers left after one month, but the civilians stayed behind. They planted crops and named their new home Corn Island after the abundant corn crop.

George Rogers Clark

As the civilians were settling on Corn Island, French King Louis XVI sent troops and supplies to help the Americans fight against the British. The following year, on April 17, 1779, the Corn Island civilians crossed the river and established a new town. To thank France for helping out, they named the town Louisville, after King Louis XVI. And because in French, the name "Louis" is pronounced LOO-ee, the city is called LOO-ee-vill! (More on that over on page 54!).

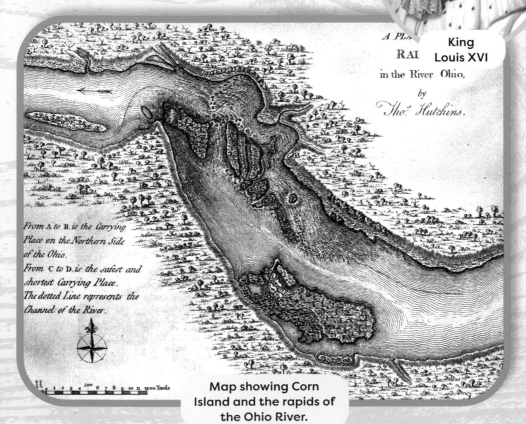

King Louis XVI

A PLA
RAI
in the River Ohio,
by
Tho.ˢ Hutchins.

From A to B. is the Carrying Place on the Northern Side of the Ohio.
From C to D. is the safest and shortest Carrying Place.
The dotted Line represents the Channel of the River.

500
0 1 2 3 4   6 7 8 9 10 11 1200 Yards

Map showing Corn Island and the rapids of the Ohio River.

The Falls of the Ohio

The rushing water that became the Ohio River started gushing over a large area of rock to the west of Louisville more than 300 million years ago. Eventually, the water scrubbed away the soil, forming the river and exposing ancient fossil beds. The river also cascaded down a series of steep cliffs, forming what is known today as the Falls of the Ohio. This famous stretch of water moves between Louisville, Kentucky, and Clarksville, Indiana. Today, it's part of a protected wildlife conservation area and popular for fishing, birdwatching, boating, biking, and hiking.

Early Days: Underwater limestone formations created shallow waters where the river slowed down. This area was the perfect place for bison and Indigenous peoples to cross the river. When settlers came in the late 1700s, though, their cargo boats ran aground in the shallows. They had to stop, unload their cargo, and carry it over land to the far side of the Falls. Then it was reloaded onto new boats before the settlers could continue on their way to the Mississippi River.

Lock 'Em Up: To avoid some of that overland travel, locks were added to the river starting in 1825. Locks are boxes that hold back the water and allow people to raise or lower the water level. A boat enters the lock, and the water is raised or lowered to match the water height of the next section of the river. Then the box is opened, and the boat can continue its journey. Canals and dams were added later to further control the mighty river.

HISTORY: First People

10,000 to 7,000 BCE: The first people in Kentucky arrived at the end of the last Ice Age, following herds of large animals, like mammoth and bison. Few artifacts from this time survive except for spear points and tools used for cutting, chopping, and scraping.

7,000 to 1,000 BCE: As the climate warmed, large animals died off, so people hunted small animals like deer, turkey, and rabbit. Archaeologists have found spear points, axes, and throwing tools called atl-atls (right). Burial sites with shells have also been found in Kentucky.

1,000 BCE to 1000: During this period, people lived in more permanent homes. They grew vegetables, like sunflowers and squash, and also grew and smoked tobacco. Archaeologists have found spear points, arrowheads, tools, and pottery shards in digs and mounds (right) near the Ohio River.

1000 to 1700: The Mississippian people lived west of the Falls, and Fort Ancient people lived east of the Falls. Both peoples used arrows and spears, as well as European weapons, like rifles. Archaeologists have found pottery jars, bowls, plates, bottles, and colanders.

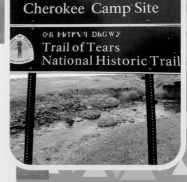

1700s: Historians are split about whether Indigenous people had many permanent settlements during this period in what is now Kentucky. Most agree that the land was mainly used for hunting and trapping rather than for villages. By the late 1700s, though, white settlers met with visitors from the Miami, Wyandot, Shawnee, and Seneca peoples, among others. Most of the Indigenous people arrived in the area from elsewhere in the south or Midwest.

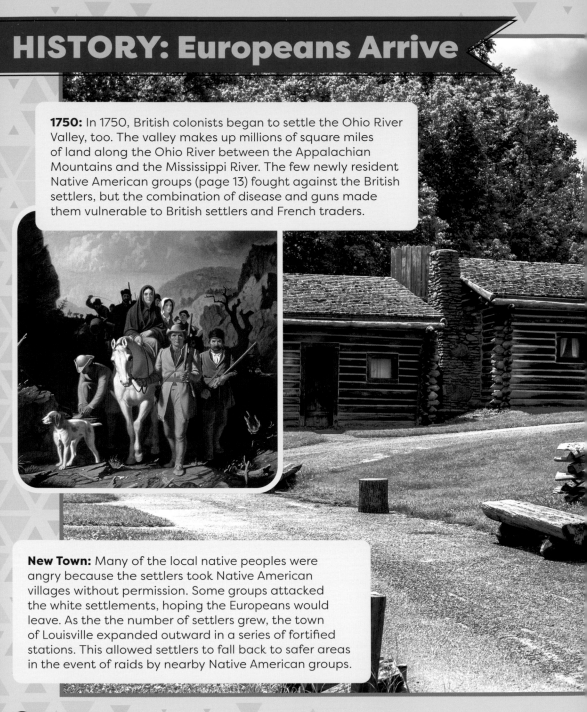

1750: In 1750, British colonists began to settle the Ohio River Valley, too. The valley makes up millions of square miles of land along the Ohio River between the Appalachian Mountains and the Mississippi River. The few newly resident Native American groups (page 13) fought against the British settlers, but the combination of disease and guns made them vulnerable to British settlers and French traders.

New Town: Many of the local native peoples were angry because the settlers took Native American villages without permission. Some groups attacked the white settlements, hoping the Europeans would leave. As the the number of settlers grew, the town of Louisville expanded outward in a series of fortified stations. This allowed settlers to fall back to safer areas in the event of raids by nearby Native American groups.

15th State: Kentucky became the 15th state on June 1, 1792.

Slavery in Kentucky: Before statehood, Kentucky was part of Virginia, the state with the largest population of enslaved people. This meant that many British/American settlers were slaveholders who brought enslaved people with them. Kentucky's first constitution in 1792 protected the rights of slaveholders. (Because Indiana and Ohio, to the north, were always free states, many enslaved people came through Louisville between 1810 and 1860 via the Underground Railroad, an escape system of hideouts and pathways to freedom.)

SLAVE TRADING IN LOUISVILLE

By the 1850s, Kentucky was annually exporting between 2500 and 4000 of its slaves down river to the large plantations farther south. To prevent runaways, traders operating near the Ohio River kept slaves shackled together in pens when not being displayed to buyers. Slave traders were often social outcasts avoided by all but fellow traders.

HISTORY: From the Civil War to World War II

Civil War (1861–1865): As a border state between the Union and the Confederacy (the opposing sides in the Civil War), Kentucky was deeply divided over which side to support. Ultimately, Kentucky sided with the North. It remained a free state in the Union. Because the city was right on the Ohio River, Louisville was important to the Union Army, with forts, barracks, and storage for supplies.

FAST FACT
The first Kentucky Derby was held in 1875. A horse named Aristides was the winner!

Reconstruction (1865-1880): After the Civil War ended with a Union victory, many formerly enslaved people moved to Louisville, which already had the nation's largest established community of free Black people. The population of the city grew enormously overall, as well.

Post-Reconstruction (1880-1918): In 1900, Louisville had a population of 200,000 and was the 18th largest city in the nation. It was a center for manufacturing and transportation. During this period, Kentucky passed laws to make life better for its citizens. These included laws that helped protect child workers and made workplaces and housing safer.

World War I: Built in just 69 days in 1917, when the United States entered World War I in Europe, Camp Zachary Taylor trained 150,000 men. It was the training camp for the 84th Army Division.

World War II: From 1941 to 1945, Louisville manufacturers helped fight the war from home. The Ford Motor Company factory began to build military Jeeps instead of family cars. Factories in the Rubbertown area produced about a quarter of the country's synthetic rubber, used for tires and machine parts both in the war and at home.

Despite siding with the North in the Civil War, Kentucky has dealt with issues of racial discrimination. Kentucky was a "free" state before the Civil War, but it was far from perfect in its treatment of Black Americans after the war. Here are some key stories from the ongoing struggle for equal rights. You can find historical markers in the city honoring these people and events.

FAST FACT

Hunt for historic Civil Rights History Trail markers in downtown Louisville. The 11 markers were created by sculptor Ed Hamilton.

Zion Baptist: In 1877, a group of African Americans formed the Zion Baptist Church. It became an important hub for the African American community in Louisville. The congregation grew large enough that the church eventually moved to its current home on Muhammad Ali Blvd.

Black Newspaper: In 1917, I. Willis Cole used his $50 savings to start "The Louisville Leader," a weekly newspaper for the African American community. The newspaper promoted desegregation and public education for African American children. The newspaper was popular and remained in publication until shortly after Mr. Cole's death in 1950.

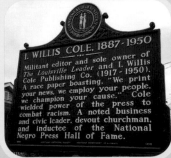

Library Sit-In: In 1941, Murray Atkins Walls participated in a sit-in at the main library of Louisville's Free Public Library. Her goal was to end racial segregation in public libraries. She also fought for desegregation of public schools in the state, and she helped to desegregate local Girl Scout camps in 1954.

Murray Atkins Walls

Integrated University: In 1951, the Louisville Municipal College for Negroes merged with the University of Louisville, finally making that school fully integrated. The first Black professor at the University of Louisville was Dr. Charles H. Parrish, Jr., whose father had been born into slavery. Dr. Parrish was a community activist who promoted education for all children.

Fair Housing Struggles: In 1954, the Wade family, who were Black, decided to challenge housing segregation in Louisville. Their friends, the Bradens, who were white, bought a house and then transferred ownership of the house to the Wades. The Wades moved into their new house. Within the first two months, it was shot at and bombed, and a cross was burned across the street. Mr. Braden was accused of being a communist and arrested and jailed. Eventually, the Wades moved back to their former neighborhood. These events pushed the government to pass the Fair Housing Act in 1968.

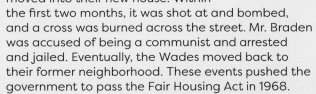

Boycotts: In 1961, young people in Louisville and many other Southern cities led nonviolent demonstrations to end racial segregation, including sit-ins and marches. Many protesters were arrested. The best known protest in Louisville was called "Nothing New for Easter." Black people boycotted stores by refusing to buy new clothes for Easter. By the summer of 1961, most businesses in Louisville had been desegregated.

Secretariat: On May 5, 1973, Secretariat won the Kentucky Derby with the fastest race time ever, 1 minute, 59 2/5 seconds, a record that still stands (through 2022). Secretariat went on to win the Triple Crown (winning two other famous horse races: the Preakness and the Belmont Stakes), and is considered one of the best racehorses ever.

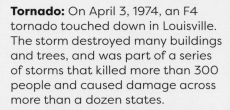

Tornado: On April 3, 1974, an F4 tornado touched down in Louisville. The storm destroyed many buildings and trees, and was part of a series of storms that killed more than 300 people and caused damage across more than a dozen states.

Look! Up in the Sky!: The first "Thunder Over Louisville" was held more than 30 years ago, featuring a high-speed air show, rivercraft demonstrations, live music, food, and one of the most (shall we say) explosive fireworks shows in the country! Read more about this only-in-Louisville mega-event on page 36.

Waterfront Park: On July 4, 1999, Waterfront Park (background) officially opened. The park has walking trails and a playground and hosts outdoor events. With views of the river and beautiful bridges, it is now a centerpiece of life in Louisville, and a regular stop for visitors.

David Armstrong Extreme Park: On April 5, 2002, the David Armstrong Extreme Park opened. Considered one of the best skate parks in the US, it's got everything from bowls to a street course to a 24-foot full-pipe!

4th Street Live!: On June 1, 2004, 4th Street Live! opened. It is located in downtown Louisville and has businesses, restaurants, and shops, as well as outdoor concerts.

People from the Past!

Meet some interesting people from Louisville's past.

Zachary Taylor (1784–1850)

Taylor was the 12th President of the United States. He was born when the town of Louisville was only five years old. His parents moved to a farm east of Louisville when he was a baby. When he grew up, he joined the Army and fought in the War of 1812 and in the Mexican War. He died in 1850 of stomach problems, only 16 months after he was elected President. Vice President Millard Fillmore took over from Taylor as president.

Charles W. Anderson, Jr. (1907–1960)

Born in Louisville, Anderson was a lawyer and elected official who spent his life fighting for rights for Black people in Kentucky. In 1935, he became the first Black person elected to the Kentucky House of Representatives. He helped pass laws to give more educational opportunities to Black children, improve working conditions, and raise the minimum wage. He even helped pass a law allowing married women to be teachers. Shortly before he died, President Eisenhower appointed him to the United Nations as a delegate in 1959.

Anne Braden (1924–2006)

Anne Braden was a Civil Rights activist and a journalist. She was born in Louisville in 1924. While she worked as a journalist, she fought for desegregation and labor rights. Dr. Martin Luther King, Jr., even mentioned her in his Letter from a Birmingham Jail, calling her "eloquent and prophetic." Anne Braden was accused of being a communist because of her Civil Rights activism, but lived to see much of her hard work pay off.

Mae Street Kidd (1904–1999)

Mae Street Kidd was born in 1904 into a biracial family. She was elected to the Kentucky General Assembly where her colleagues called her the "Lady of the House." She fought for rights for fair housing, civil rights, and opportunities for children and poor people. In 1976, more than 100 years after the Civil War, Kentucky still hadn't ratified (or made legal or official) the 13th, 14th, and 15th Amendments (laws that gave equal voting and citizenship rights to formerly enslaved people). Kidd thought that was shameful. With her help, those Amendments were finally ratified in Kentucky.

Favorite Son: Muhammad Ali

Heavyweight boxing champion. Peace activist. Humanitarian. And Louisville's most famous citizen: Muhammad Ali.

Louisville Years: Muhammad Ali was born Cassius Clay in 1942 in a segregated neighborhood in Louisville. He started boxing at a local gym when he was 13, and soon became a skilled boxer. In 1960, the same year he graduated from high school, he won the Olympic gold medal in light-heavyweight boxing. Four years later, he became the world heavyweight champion.

Name Change: In 1964, soon after he won the heavyweight title, Clay announced that he had become a Muslim, joined the Nation of Islam, and changed his name to Muhammad Ali. Almost overnight, he went from being a national hero to a disliked figure. But he stuck to his principles. In 1967, he refused to enter the Army draft for the Vietnam War, saying his faith believed in peace. He had his heavyweight title taken away and was even convicted of a crime (the charge was later overturned). Though he missed out on boxing for almost three years, Ali finally came back and won the title again.

The Champ: Ali became revered for his beliefs and his conviction, and he used his fame to help many people. His outgoing personality and athletic success made him an international icon. Ali retired in 1981 when he was 39 years old. He was the only person to win the heavyweight title three times.

Struggles: In the years after he left the ring, Ali developed Parkinson's syndrome. The nerve disorder, probably brought on by being hit in the head while boxing, slowed his movements and mostly silenced his powerful voice. But Ali still traveled to promote peace, becoming a beloved figure around the world.

Roots: Ali never forgot his roots in Louisville. His home there is now a museum about his life, and in 2005, Ali and his wife, Lonnie, opened the Muhammad Ali Center. Located on Museum Row, the center is a place for young people to visit and learn about Ali's six core principles: confidence, conviction, dedication, giving, respect, and spirituality.

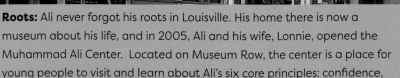

Louisville Today

Louisville started out as a frontier fort, but in the last 250 years it has grown into the largest city in Kentucky. Check out some more fun things Louisville is known for!

Gateway to the South: Louisville is sometimes called the Gateway to the South because of its location. Because its a short drive to seven boundary states (Indiana, Illinois, Missouri, Tennessee, Virginia, West Virginia, and Ohio), Louisville is considered a bridge between the Midwest and the South.

Parks: From wilderness parks, to river or creekside parks, to playgrounds, Louisville has parks for everyone. There are parks for skateboarders, hikers, dogs, and children. There's definitely a park for you!

Louisville Dog Run Association

Sawyer Dog Park

E.P. "Tom" Sawyer State Park: Archery, astronomy, orienteering, BMX racing, dogs, birding—these are just a few of the things to do here.

The Highlands: If food is your thing, you'll want to stroll along Bardstown Road to find the perfect restaurant for you. From pizza places to breakfast spots to casual dining, you're sure to find a restaurant you like. And while you're looking, be sure to stop in at one of the local shops to find a one-of-a-kind souvenir!

The Kentucky Derby

Since 1875, the first Saturday in May, known in Louisville as Derby Day, includes "the most exciting two minutes in sports." After all, the Kentucky Derby is the most famous horse race in the world! Every year, more than 140,000 people pack the stands at the Churchill Downs racetrack, which opened way back in 1875. While the 1.25-mile Derby race around the one-mile-long dirt oval is over quickly, there's lots to do and see on Derby Day, from the amazing hats to a full day of other races.

FAST FACT
The Kentucky Derby is the longest continually running sports event in the country.

The field of horses bursts out of the gate at the Kentucky Derby.

Hats!

While the horses are the stars of the show at the Kentucky Derby, the people watching the race put on a show, too. Women and men dress to impress, often showing off huge, colorful, creative hats of all kinds. The fashion parade off the track lasts longer than the race, as people walk around to see and be seen.

Race Info

➤ Horses can only run one time in the Kentucky Derby—the year they are three years old.

➤ Most horses that run in the Derby are male, but fillies (female horses) can run, too.

➤ As many as 20 horses compete in each Kentucky Derby.

The Kentucky Derby

More Than a Race

Louisvillians and horse-racing fans from around the world put on their most colorful "going out" clothes and head to Churchill Downs. Along with the Derby, there is music, at least 11 other races, great food, traditional drinks, and lots and lots of selfies!

FAST FACT
The event is also called the "Run for the Roses" for the blanket of flowers draped on the winning horse.

Derby Heroes

➤ **Secretariat (1973)** Triple Crown winner who set a Derby record of (1:59.40) that still stands today.

➤ **Eddie Arcaro and Bill Hartack** each rode five winners, tied for most ever.

➤ **Seattle Slew (1977)** won the Derby and then the Triple Crown, and never lost a single race.

➤ **American Pharaoh (2015)** was the most recent horse to win the Triple Crown (through 2022).

➤ **Rich Strike (2022)** was the biggest longshot (80 to 1) to win the Derby.

Rich Strike

Things to see in Louisville

If this is your first visit to Louisville, here are some places you'll definitely want to check out:

Blackacre State Nature Preserve

The preserve is home to one of the oldest trees in Kentucky—a white oak tree that was a sapling in 1696! You can walk around Blackacre's 300 acres and look at that tree and other natural wonders from observation decks and trails. The Community Garden is where locals can rent a plot to grow their own tomatoes and cucumbers. And Blackacre's homestead building is more than 200 years old. Tour old houses and barns, and learn about Kentucky's role in the American Revolution.

Not Just for People

In Louisville with your best friend? Try a dog park! Visit the Barklands of Floyds Fork, Sawyer Dog Park, with a special section just for small dogs, or Waverly Dog Run, which has trails through a wooded area.

Things to See in Louisville

Jefferson Memorial Forest: Ready for camping in the city? Jefferson Memorial Forest has campsite rentals where you can sleep after spending the day hiking or fishing. The forest is more than 6,000 acres. Visit the Welcome Center to find books, trail guides, and supplies.

Cave Hill Cemetery: A cemetery as a tourist spot? Sure, why not! More than 100,000 people have been buried in Cave Hill Cemetery since 1848. You can tour the cemetery to see burial sites and beautiful sculptures. Some famous people buried here:

➤ George Rogers Clark—built a fort in Louisville during the American Revolution (top).

➤ Colonel Harland Sanders is best known for his special secret recipe for fried chicken. You'd know his chicken recipe as Kentucky Fried Chicken (middle).

➤ Senator Georgia Powers was the first Black person and first woman elected to the Kentucky State Senate.

➤ Susan Look Avery was a suffragist who fought for equal rights for all women regardless of race.

➤ Pretty Polly is a parrot who is the only animal buried here.

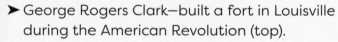

Waterfront Park Botanical Gardens: Just a short walk from downtown Louisville is the city's crown jewel. Waterfront Park Botanical Gardens has walking paths along the river with pools, waterfalls, and green spaces perfect for picnicking and flying kites. There is a natural parkland area with a variety of pollinators, birds, and other animals, and a playground for children of all ages.

The **Big Four Pedestrian Bridge** is an old railroad bridge that was turned into a bridge for walkers and bicyclists. Pedestrians can see kayakers in the river below as they walk above the Ohio River from Louisville to Indiana.

Old Louisville: No visit to Louisville is complete without taking the walking tour of "haunted" Victorian mansions in Old Louisville, which also includes the area around the University of Louisville. Nearby Freedom Park has a series of memorials commemorating Louisville's fight for civil rights.

Things to See in Louisville

The Parklands of Floyds Fork: This system of natural parks takes up about 4,000 acres in Louisville. It includes a woodland garden, hiking paths, and playground with water features, all along Floyds Fork.

The Little Loomhouse: Take a historic tour of the Little Loomhouse to learn about weaving and fiber arts. While you're there, be sure to learn about Mildred Jane Hill and Patty Smith Hill, the sisters who wrote "Happy Birthday to You."

The Highlands: Head down "Restaurant Row," especially in the morning to get breakfast at one of the many breakfast spots. And while you're there, you won't want to miss Carmichaels Bookstore, Louisville's oldest independent bookstore. You can grab signed copies of books, and maybe even catch an author signing.

The Kentucky Derby Museum

Learn all about the Run for the Roses at the Kentucky Derby Museum. Check out family-friendly interactive exhibits. In Riders Up, you can ride in a simulated horse race. Learn about famous horses like American Pharaoh and Secretariat and their impact on racing. Visit the Derby Museum Stable and horse around with some new friends, like Mighty "Ari" Aristides, a miniature horse named for the first winner of the Kentucky Derby in 1875. (Yes, he even has his own TikTok account.)

Gheens Science Hall and Rauch Planetarium

There is so much to see at the planetarium. Climb aboard a virtual spaceship and tour the galaxy. Learn about the solar system in planetarium workshops. Watch a star and laser show. You'll find Gheens Science Hall and Rauch Planetarium on the University of Louisville campus.

Riverside

Along a thirteen-mile stretch on the banks of the Ohio River south of Louisville is the history-packed Farnsley-Moremen Landing at Riverside. See an old-time farmhouse, and check out excavations near the outbuildings. Archaeologists have dated artifacts back to 1830. They say that Riverside's artifacts are teaching them about life in the 1800s, especially the daily life of enslaved people.

Locust Grove

Locust Grove was home to William and Lucy Clark Croghan. William Croghan arrived in Louisville with George Rogers Clark in 1778 to scout the Ohio River Valley during the American Revolution. He later married Clark's sister Lucy. They started building the house at Locust Grove around 1792. Locust Grove is now owned by Jefferson County and is open to the public.

Tarzan in Louisville

Remember that old phrase "Don't judge a book by its cover"? That's true of the book-filled Ekstrom Library on the University of Louisville campus. From the outside, it looks just like any other library. But on the lower level of the library is the Rare Books Room. Among the treasures is one of the largest collections of the works of Edgar Rice Burroughs—yes, the guy who wrote the Tarzan stories starting in 1912.

Kentucky Kingdom

Rollercoasters, waterslides, and dog shows, oh my! This awesome amusement park is packed with wild rides and thrills galore. You can go round and round, upside down, or into a spin! The huge park also includes Hurricane Bay, a waterpark, so pack your suit and plan to get wet!

Thunder Over Louisville

Like fireworks? You won't want to miss **Thunder over Louisville**! Thunder started in 1988 as part of the Kentucky Derby Festival. It was a huge show even then—10,000 people showed up! Today it is the largest fireworks show in the country.

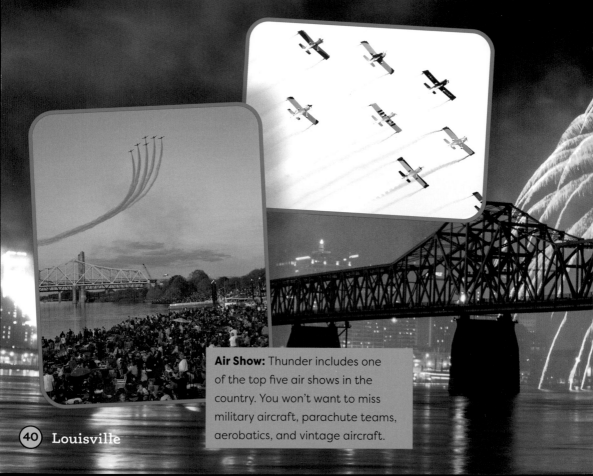

Air Show: Thunder includes one of the top five air shows in the country. You won't want to miss military aircraft, parachute teams, aerobatics, and vintage aircraft.

More Than Explosions: Thunder has family events all day at Waterfront Park, including interactive displays, fun zones, and tons of kids activities (think face painting, bounce houses, mini golf, and more!). And when everybody's stomach starts thundering for lunch, Thunder's FoodFest has the whole family covered. With more than 100 food vendors, there's literally something for everyone!

Weather: Four Seasons in Louisville

Is there a best time to visit Louisville? Depending on when you visit, you might experience snow in winter, cool rain in spring, humidity and heat in summer, or crisp air in autumn. Louisville's weather can change from sunny skies to pouring rain in just a few minutes. That's why folks in Kentucky say, "If you don't like the weather, just wait 15 minutes."

Winter: Winter is beautiful in Louisville. Temperatures stay around 30 degrees—cold enough to get some good snowfalls, but not super freezing like some midwestern or northern cities. During winter, you can skate at an outdoor ice rink, sled at one of Louisville's many parks, or even take a Polar Bear Plunge in the Ohio River to help raise money for the Special Olympics.

Spring: Spring brings warming temperatures, wildflowers, and the Kentucky Derby Festival. Temperatures mostly stay around 50 degrees— perfect outdoor weather. But watch out for mud! Melting winter snow and spring rain make Louisville's parks and waterfront areas muddy.

Summer: Summer in Louisville can range from sunny 70 degrees to humid and hot in the 80s or even 90s. Believe it or not, summer is almost as rainy as spring. Pack an umbrella or find the nearest doorway or park shelter to duck under until rainstorms pass. Summer is perfect for outdoor fun. Picnicking. Hiking. Boating. Bicycling. Camping. Swimming.

Fall: The cool fall weather is a break from summer heat. Temperatures stay around 60 degrees—beautiful outdoor weather. Check out nearby farms for apple picking, pumpkin hunting, and petting zoos. Old-fashioned train rides, harvest festivals, and corn mazes are just a few fun fall activities in Louisville.

GETTING AROUND
LOUISVILLE

Most people in Louisville get around by car, but check out some other ways to get from one part of Louisville to another.

LouVelo : Want to bicycle around Louisville but don't have your own bike? No worries! LouVelo has you covered. This bike share is pay as you go, and with more than 30 stations, picking up and dropping off a bike is easy.

TARC : Louisville's bus system, Transit Authority of River City, has routes all over the metro area. You'll want to plan your trip, though, to make sure you take the right connections to get where you're going.

Louisville Loop : The Loop's paths are shared-use paths for bicyclists and pedestrians (and their pets!). When completed, the Loop will have more than 100 miles of trails circling and connecting parks and neighborhoods in the city.

Belle of Louisville

If you'd like to see Louisville from the Ohio River, there's no better way than aboard the *Belle of Louisville* or her sister ship the *Mary M. Miller*. The Belle is the oldest operating steamboat in America. She's over 100 years old! There are many different riverboat trips to take. Options include dinner cruises, kid cruises, and special events, like the Roaring 20s Sunset Cruise or the Swashbuckling Family Adventure. The *Mary M. Miller* is a propeller-driven riverboat. She's *Belle's* much younger sister—built in 1985.

FAST FACT
The Mary M. Miller is named after Mary Millicent Miller, America's first woman steamboat captain.

Museums— Go See 'Em!

Art, history, science, sports—there's a museum for everyone in Louisville.

Frazier Kentucky History Museum : The Frazier is the best place to see collections of Kentucky artifacts. You will find toys, clothing, and historical documents, including an arrest warrant for Mary Todd Lincoln (President Abraham Lincoln's wife) from March 1875. (Back then, a person could be sent to a mental hospital by a court. Mrs. Lincoln was arrested and convicted, but let out of the hospital a few months later.) The Frazier also has a collection of old weapons and miniature toy soldiers, some going back to the 1700s.

Museum of the American Printing House for the Blind : A visit to this museum will inspire you. It includes the stories of blind and sighted people who fought for fairness and accessibility. When you tour the museum, you can learn how Braille books and talking books are made. The museum also includes many objects from the archive of Helen Keller, famous for living a long, creative, and influential life even though she could not see or hear.

Helen Keller

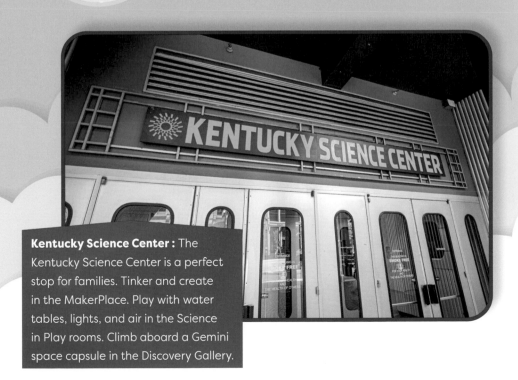

Kentucky Science Center : The Kentucky Science Center is a perfect stop for families. Tinker and create in the MakerPlace. Play with water tables, lights, and air in the Science in Play rooms. Climb aboard a Gemini space capsule in the Discovery Gallery.

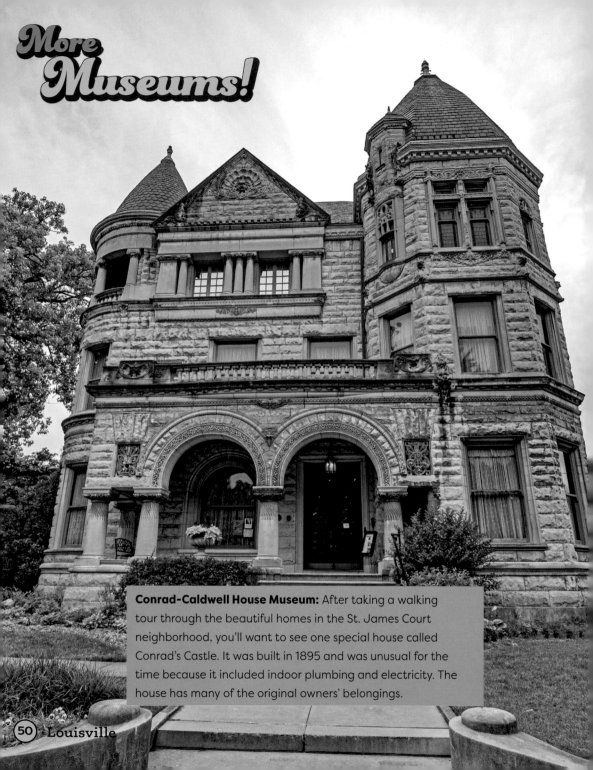

More Museums!

Conrad-Caldwell House Museum: After taking a walking tour through the beautiful homes in the St. James Court neighborhood, you'll want to see one special house called Conrad's Castle. It was built in 1895 and was unusual for the time because it included indoor plumbing and electricity. The house has many of the original owners' belongings.

Roots 101: African-American Museum: Attend a poetry slam. View exhibits, like "Faces of Africa," "Big Momma's House," or "Roots of African-American Music." Learn about the contributions and experiences of African Americans in Kentucky and elsewhere in the United States.

Creative Glass: If you time your visit right, you'll catch glassblowers at work at Flame Run. Watch from the balcony as glass artists here handle 2000-degree melted glass and turn it into beautiful works of art! Also check out the Payton Glass Activity Center: Watch artists create, plus learn how to cut glass and make your own art in the Fuse It! Workshop.

Louisville Slugger
Museum and Factory

What is a Louisville Slugger? It's a baseball bat! Since 1884, the most famous bats in the sport have been made here. Many top players even have their own special size of Louisville Slugger. A tour of the museum includes a look at the Signature Wall where you can see a collection of ballplayers' signatures—the same ones burned onto their bats.

Along with seeing how bats are made (see box), you can practice your swing in Bud's Batting Cage or try out bats of famous players like Babe Ruth or Jackie Robinson. Take it one step further in the Hold a Piece of History exhibit where you can hold bats actually used by famous players.

The Bat Vault holds some old bats—up to 100 years old! Learn about the different bats players used and how they improved their swing. You can see Babe Ruth's notched bat (yes, he really did carve those notches himself!), Joe DiMaggio's 56 game hit streak bat, and Hank Aaron's 700th home run bat.

FAST FACT

The museum is home to the biggest baseball bat in the world. It is made of steel and stands 120 feet tall!. Two doors down, look for a giant baseball busting through a window at a mirror and glass company.

Making a Bat

In the Factory part of the tour, see the five steps that go into making a Slugger.

➤ Louisville Sluggers are made from wood from white ash and maple trees.

➤ Cut trees are sent to mills where the timber is cut into long cylinders.

➤ At the factory, the wooden cylinders are shaved and cut to exact measurements for each bat.

➤ The bats are then painted or varnished, and the Slugger logo and player name are burned into the wood.

At the end of the tour, everyone gets their very own mini Louisville Slugger bat!

Outdoor Art

Love in the Street : Poet and artist Lance Newman collected poems from Louisvillians. The love poems to Louisville were stamped into sidewalks in downtown Louisville. The 21 poems were written by poets from age 3 to 80.

Charles H. Parrish, Jr. Freedom Park: Walk along the path of Freedom Park and read stories of Black people in Louisville who challenged racism and fought for equal rights. You'll find information panels at this park on the campus of University of Louisville.

Outdoor Murals:
You'll also want to hunt for the murals painted onto the walls of buildings in downtown Louisville. Try to find the artists' signatures on their giant paintings.

Art Museums

Kentucky Museum of Art and Craft: Try to make it to one of KMAC's Family Fun Days if you can. You'll see pop-up tours and artist demonstrations and make your own art to take home. If you can't make it to a Family Fun Day, KMAC offers art and craft exhibits and creator space projects year-round.

Speed Art Museum : If you spend an afternoon touring the University of Louisville, you'll want to stop in at the Speed Art Museum, right on campus. After you see the Speed's art collection, stop in the Open Studio to create art of your own.

Paul Paletti Gallery : Fans of photography will want to check out this gallery's changing exhibitions of historic and contemporary photographs. Best time to visit? Paul Paletti Gallery participates in the First Friday Trolley Hop, a weekly event that takes visitors to Louisville art galleries on a free trolley!

21C Louisville : Here you might find interactive art, like *Text Rain* by Camille Utterback, or the 30-foot-tall *David (inspired by Michelangelo)* by Serkan Ozkaya.

Embroiderer's Guild of America : The guild's headquarters is in Louisville, and you can visit on weekdays to view the permanent exhibits. The headquarters is home to The National Tapestry: America the Beautiful, a five-year-long project created by members of the guild. You can also visit the lending library, take classes, and make free projects.

How to SAY Louisville

If you walk down a street in Louisville and ask folks how to say the name of their city, you'll get a bunch of different answers.

Looeyville
(LOO-ee-vil)

Looavul
(LOO-uh-vul)

Luhvul
(LOO-vul)

Loueville
(LOO-eh-vil)

Looaville
(LOO-uh-vil)

And the Winner Is . . .

According to the Louisville Tourist Commission the right way to say it is the French way: LOO-ee-vill. After all, Louisville was named for French King Louis XVI.

But that's not the final answer! If you want to sound like a local, you'll probably want to pronounce it LOO-uh-vul.

How to TALK Louisville

Calm your horses
Everyone, just calm down.

Fixin' to
Getting ready to do something.

I reckon
I guess.

Buggy
The rest of the country calls this a shopping cart.

Yonder
Over there.

Fair to middling
If someone asks you how you're doing, you might answer "fair to middling," meaning "I'm okay."

Fast time, slow time
Louisville is right on the edge of the time zone change between the Eastern Time Zone and the Central Time Zone. "Fast time" and "slow time" are sometimes used instead of "Eastern" or "Central."

Fort Knox

South of downtown Louisville is an amazing building filled with gold! Really! The US Mint runs the Gold Bullion Depository at a huge building . . . that, of course, you cannot visit. But you can drive by and see a place that holds 140 million ounces of gold (worth more than $190 billion!), all stacked in seven-inch-long bars. Since 1937, Fort Knox has been home to most of the gold owned by the United States government.

What's in a Fort? Soldiers!

Surrounding the gold building is a huge US Army base. Thousands of soldiers live and train there. Some learn to drive tanks, others are working to become infantry soldiers. Many Army soldiers spend weeks or months here before being transferred to duty stations around the world.

A Place to Visit

The General George Patton Museum is at Fort Knox . . . and you can visit that, at least. It includes stories of his long career, as well as information about World War I and World War II. You can see Army vehicles and gear from throughout the 20th century.

LOUISVILLE: It's Weird!

Louisville is the disco ball capital of the world. Ninety percent of the disco balls produced in America are made in Louisville.

Visit the Louisville Mega Cavern to try out underground zip lining. It's the largest building in the state of Kentucky with 17 miles of corridors. And it's entirely underground!

The first successful hand transplant in the United States happened in Louisville in 1999.

Best tap water in the country? Louisville's tap water won the People's Choice competition for the best tap water. Visit Water Tower Park to learn more about Louisville's water—and taste it for yourself!

Jennifer Lawrence

Jennifer Lawrence started her acting career when she was a teenager. By her early twenties, she starred in *The Hunger Games* movies and *X-Men: First Class*. She won several awards for her performance in *Silver Linings Playbook*, including an Academy Award and a Golden Globe Award among others.

Ed Hamilton

Voted "Louisvillian of the Year" in 2020, Ed Hamilton is a Louisville icon. He is best known for his sculptures of famous people, like Martin Luther King, Jr., and Abraham Lincoln. His work sits in public spaces, and he has won many awards and honors. Some of his public art is on display in Louisville, like *The Abraham Lincoln Memorial at Waterfront Plaza* and his *Memorial to Honor York*.

What People Do in LOUISVILLE

Just under 400,000 people live in Louisville. Here are some things they do:

Yum Brands's headquarters is in Louisville. It's one of the biggest fast-food companies in the world. You might have heard of some of their restaurants: KFC, Pizza Hut, Taco Bell, and The Habit Burger Grill.

UPS has its Air Operations headquarters in Louisville. At the Louisville Air Hub, UPS employees sort 416,000 packages/documents per hour. Packages that fly out of Louisville travel to more than 200 countries and territories around the world.

Louisville muhammad Ali International Airport:

When the airport opened in 1947, it was called Standiford Field. Since the 1990s, it has been home to the Kentucky Air National Guard Base and a United States Postal Service air mail facility.

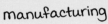

Health Care

The healthcare industry is one of the fastest growing industries in Louisville. It employs more than 57,000 people.

manufacturing

Louisville is home to many different types of manufacturing, including automobiles, appliances, and glass. more than 80,000 people in Louisville are employed in manufacturing jobs.

Eat the Louisville Way

There are plenty of places to eat in Louisville, from restaurant chains you know to local restaurants. While you're there, try out these Louisville specialties! You could even join a food and history walking tour! (Yum!)

Hot Brown: Like messy sandwiches? Then you'll love the Hot Brown. It's an open-faced sandwich with turkey, bacon, tomatoes, sauce, and parmesan cheese. It was first served at the Brown Hotel in Louisville in the 1920s.

Benedictine Sandwich: For a less messy sandwich, try the Benedictine Sandwich. The sandwich spread is made by mixing cream cheese and cucumbers. You can add more cucumbers or even bacon on top of the spread, if you'd like. Benedictine spread was first made by Jennie C. Benedict in the early 1900s.

Modjeska: If you prefer a sweet treat, you might like Modjeska candies. The candies have a marshmallow center surrounded by caramel. They were first made by Anton Busath in the 1880s. Mr. Busath named them after a famous actress, Madam Modjeska.

Derby-Pie: And for an even sweeter treat, you won't want to miss Derby-Pie. Derby-Pies have been made by Kern's Kitchen since 1954. The recipe is top secret, but it features a flaky crust and a creamy mix of chocolate and walnuts.

Go, Louisville Sports!

RACING LOUISVILLE FOOTBALL CLUB

Joined the National Women's Soccer League in 2021.

Cool Stuff: Racing Louisville FC became the first major league sports team in Louisville in more than 40 years.

➤ Its academy trains kids as young as 3 years old all the way up to 18 years old.

Big Names: Emily Fox, Savannah McCaskill, Jess McDonald

Home: Lynn Family Stadium

UNIVERSITY OF LOUISVILLE CARDINALS

Joined the Atlantic Coast Conference in 2014, but have been playing football since 1912

Cool Stuff: The Cardinals have won three NCAA basketball championships and eight football conference championships

➤ The women's volleyball team had a perfect season in 2021!

➤ The Ladybirds Dance Team has earned 20 national titles

Big Names: Johnny Unitas, Joe Jacoby (football); Wes Unseld, Donovan Mitchell, Angel McCoughtry (basketball)

Home: Cardinal Stadium (football); KFC Yum! Center (basketball)

The rivalry between the University of Louisville and the University of Kentucky is more than 100 years old! The big contest of the year is the men's basketball game, played every winter since 1913.

Active Louisville!

When locals are not watching sports, they're playing them . . . or at least staying active. Here are some of the ways that folks in Louisville (and Kentucky) get out and play!

The public park systems offer canoeing, kayaking, and even paddle board yoga! And the Louisville Rowing Club has two boathouses and offers engaging programs for juniors and adults alike.

Fishing is popular in Kentucky, and a great way to have fun outdoors while making lasting family memories. Anyone 16 and older must have a fishing license, but Free Fishing Days are the first Saturday and Sunday of June.

Hiking and walking trails abound in Louisville. Louisvillians love to hit the trails at Cherokee Park. The park is also a bird sanctuary, so grab your binoculars to do some birdwatching, too. Jefferson Memorial Forest has more challenging trails. Some of the best views of the countryside are seen from the tops of knobs (local slang for small hills). For a gentler woodlands hike, the Parklands of Floyds Fork show off native Kentucky trees and plants.

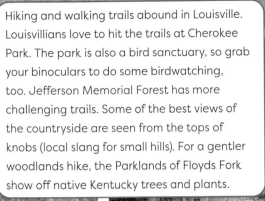

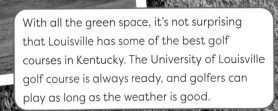

With all the green space, it's not surprising that Louisville has some of the best golf courses in Kentucky. The University of Louisville golf course is always ready, and golfers can play as long as the weather is good.

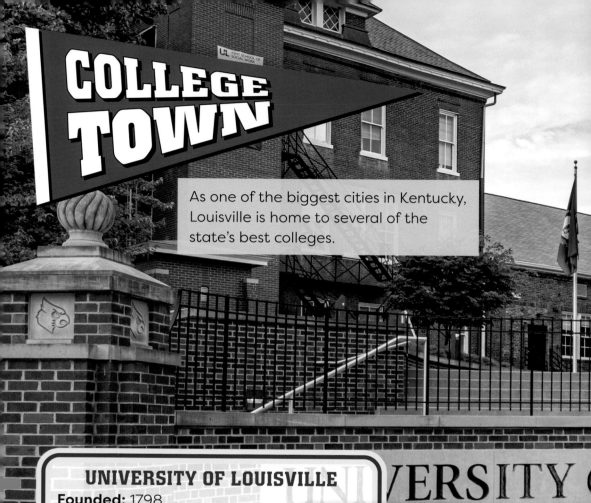

COLLEGE TOWN

As one of the biggest cities in Kentucky, Louisville is home to several of the state's best colleges.

UNIVERSITY OF LOUISVILLE

Founded: 1798
Students: 23,000
Popular Majors: Business, engineering, education, health professions
Fast Fact: The school was first called Jefferson Seminary. It changed to Louisville Medical Institute and then Louisville Collegiate Institute, before it became the University of Louisville in 1846.

UNIVERSITY OF
LOUISVILLE

SPALDING UNIVERSITY

Founded: 1814

Students: 1,600

Popular Majors: Business, fine arts, science, accounting

Fast Fact: Spalding was founded by the Sisters of Charity of Nazareth, and service to others is still an important part of the school's mission.

BELLARMINE UNIVERSITY

Founded: 1950

Students: 3,000

Popular Majors: Nursing, psychology, business, science

Fast Fact: Bellarmine was originally a school for men, but in 1968 it began admitting women and became co-educational.

SIMMONS COLLEGE OF KENTUCKY

Founded: 1879

Students: 140

Popular Majors: Religious studies, business, music, sociology

Fast Fact: Simmons College is Louisville's only HBCU (Historically Black College and University).

It's Alive!

Animals in Louisville

You might not think of wildlife when you think of big cities, but plenty of wild animals call Louisville home. With so many parks, careful watcher can find urban, forest, and river wildlife.

Urban wildlife: foxes, raccoons, bats, opossums, snakes, coyotes

River wildlife: turtles, like the Eastern box turtle, red-eared slider, river cooter

As cities expand, wild animals struggle to find homes. This is why urban parks are so important. The many urban parks in Louisville give wild animals a place to live. You can even spot bald eagles at the Parklands of Floyds Fork!

City forest wildlife:
black bears, deer

Look out for nesting turtles!

Spring is when female turtles leave rivers to dig nests for their eggs. If you're lucky enough to spot a mother turtle, stay quiet and keep your distance. You might even see her lay her eggs before she heads back to the river!

WE SAW IT AT THE ZOO

The Louisville Zoo opened in 1969. It is on 130 acres and holds more than 1,000 animals. You can visit animals in many habitats:

Gorilla

Africa: Spot Western lowland gorillas in the Gorilla Forest. Enjoy lunch in the Colobus Passageway while you watch colobus monkeys and Schmidt's red-tailed monkeys play.

FAST FACT
Black-footed ferrets are one of the most endangered mammals in the country. The Louisville Zoo has a breeding program to help increase their numbers.

Black-footed ferret

Glacier Run: Wander through Glacier Run Town and look for polar bears and grizzly bears. Learn about conservation and how to make little changes to save these beautiful animals.

Orangutan

Lynx

New Worlds: In Cats of the Americas, you can meet big cats like the lynx and puma. Try to move slooowly like the two-toed sloths.

Islands: Visit Penguin Cove and meet fairy penguins. Meet the orangutans and watch them climb and swing.

Australian Outback: Walk through Lorkeet Landing and feed birds from your hand. Hang out with friends in the Billabong Playabout.

Chameleon

HerpAquarium: Alligators, Gila monsters, and boa constrictors, oh, my! Before you leave, try out the Ropes Adventures Courses!

Spooky Sites

Some people believe in ghosts. Some people don't. Whatever you believe, you'll want to check out some of Louisville's spookiest sites.

Old Louisville is one of the most haunted neighborhoods in America. It's also one of the best preserved Victorian neighborhoods in America. Linger at one of these mansions during a walking tour of Old Louisville.

Monserrat, 851 South Fourth Street: Built in 1857 as a school and then used as a hospital during the Civil War. Today, Monserrat is an apartment building. Residents have reported that they've seen ghosts or felt like they weren't alone.

1439 South Sixth Street: Owner Susan Shearer purchased the house in 2003. Back then it was falling apart. Since then, she has been restoring it. She reports strange things happening in the house, such as knocks on windows and doors when no one is there. The radio mysteriously turns off and on. She has even seen a ghostly little girl standing on the stairs.

1464 St. James Court: Listen for the ghost gunshot! The story is that after World War II ended, a party was held here to celebrate the engagement of a young man just home from war. He wanted to shoot his pistol into the air to celebrate. The pistol misfired and the bullet killed his fiancée. Today, if you're lucky (or maybe unlucky!), you might hear a gunshot in the exact spot at the exact time of the accident so many years ago.

Festivals!

Louisville has festivals year-round. Here are just a few of the most popular ones:

Kentucky State Fair: For 10 days in August, the Kentucky State Fair features rides, concerts, and blue ribbon competitions.

Belknap Fall Festival: This street fair in October features music, food, and art.

Derby Balloon Festival: The Kentucky Derby festivities often include a balloon festival. You can even take rides in piloted balloons.

Kentuckiana Pride Festival: This 2-day festival at Big Four Bridge has live music and a parade.

Not Far Away

Heading out of town? Here are some special places to check out not too far from Louisville!

Hey! Haven't seen you in a while.

We've been visiting **Mammoth Cave!**

Hang on—that's not Louisville!

Nope! Mammoth Cave is south, heading toward Tennessee. It's the world's longest cave system—about 400 miles of it have been mapped by spelunkers!

Spelunkers????

It means cave explorers.

Whew!

The ranger led us past dripstones called the **Frozen Niagara**. We saw stalactites and stalagmites, walked up and down cave hills and narrow passages. It was wild! And dark! And a little bit scary!

Stalactites and stalagmites?

When water drips from the cave ceiling, it makes these long rock shapes. The passages started forming 2 million years ago!

They look like dripping icicles!

I know! And they're super fragile. It was amazing!!

After we visited the cave, we canoed on the **Green River**.

Was that still at Mammoth Cave?

Yep! We rested along the riverbank when we found a sandy beach area and looked for river fish.

You must have been tired after all that hiking and canoeing.

Thank goodness we got to rest for the night at a nearby campground.

Wait! Was that STILL at Mammoth Cave?!

Ha! Yes! There's a lot to do at **Mammoth Cave National Park**!

Anything else cool to see?

We went to the **Night Sky Program**. The ranger shared telescopes so we could see the moon and nearby planets. Best of all, we saw the International Space Station as it orbited overhead.

Wow! That sounds like a lot of fun!

I can't wait to go back!

Next stop, **Abe's Place**!

Abe who?

Abraham Lincoln, of course!

But you're in Kentucky!

THAT'S WHERE HE WAS BORN!

Not Illinois?

No.

His birthplace is a national park about an hour south of Louisville

Are you sure it wasn't Illinois?

YES!

Okay . . . jeez!

Along with a replica of the log cabin in he was born in, there's a **Lincoln Memorial building**.

Wait, now you're in Washington DC!

Nope . . . still Kentucky. This version of the famous memorial was built in 1910, more than a decade BEFORE the one in DC!

Kentucky 1, Washington 0!

After we left Lincoln, we did some horsing around!

Nice! And your parents let you?

They took us! We went to **Kentucky Horse Park** in Lexington.

Giddy-up!

We got to ride some really nice horses.

And there was fun campground to stay at, too.

There is also a huge horse museum, with art and history exhibits.

Hope your folks didn't have to pony up too much money.

Nice dad joke! We also got to watch some horse shows. There was even a cross-country race!

Splash! Hope that horse can swim!

LOL! It was a great way to end our trip to Kentucky!

Sister Cities Around the World

The Sister Cities Program was started after World War II as a way to encourage peaceful relationships between cities around the world. The goal of the program is for Sister Cities to cooperate and understand one another.

Perm, Russia

Leeds, England

Mainz, Germany

Montpelier, France

Adapazari, Turkey

Jiujiang, China

Tamale, Ghana

Quito, Ecuador

La Plata, Argentina

Louisville's Sister Cities

Sister Cities in Action

Here are some examples of how Louisville is working with and helping its sister cities:

Montpelier, France: Montpelier was Louisville's first Sister City. The partnership began in 1954. It makes sense that a city in France would be Louisville's first Sister City since Louisville was named in honor of King Louis XIV of France.

Tamale, Ghana: Tamale became a Louisville Sister City in 1979. Over the years, city officials from Tamale and Louisville have visited each other. Louisville has helped to build water facilities in Tamale schools.

Quito, Ecuador: Quito became Louisville's Sister City in 1962. Over the years, teachers have visited each other to take part in teacher training programs. In addition to art and ballet exchanges, Louisville has helped to provide water filtration systems and training on saving historic archives.

Books

Alexander, Kwame, and James Patterson. *Becoming Muhammad Ali.* Jimmy Patterson, 2022.

Gibson, Kevin. *Secret Louisville: A Guide to the Weird, Wonderful, and Obscure.* Reedy Press, 2017.

Magee, David. *Sweet Spot: 125 Years of Baseball and the Louisville Slugger.* Triumph, 2009.

McKee, Paul. *Kentucky Bucket List Adventure Guide: Explore 100 Offbeat Destinations You Must Visit!* Bridge Press, 2021.

Wilbur, Helen. *D Is for Derby: A Kentucky Derby Alphabet.* Sleeping Bear Press, 2014.

Web Sites

Frazier History Museum
https://www.fraziermuseum.org

Kentucky Derby Museum
https://www.derbymuseum.org

Kentucky Center for African American Heritage
https://kcaah.org

Louisville Slugger Museum
https://www.sluggermuseum.com

Louisville's official tourism site
https://www.gotolouisville.com

Photo Credits and Thanks

INDEX

Thanks for Visiting

LOUISVILLE

Come Back Soon!